YOUR BRAIN WHEN YOU'RE HAPPY

BY ABBY COLICH

BLUE OWL
BOOKS

TIPS FOR CAREGIVERS

Social and emotional learning (SEL) helps children manage emotions, learn how to feel empathy, create and achieve goals, and make good decisions. One goal of teaching SEL skills is to help children understand what is going on in their bodies and brains when they experience certain emotions. The more children understand, the more easily they may be able to regulate their emotions and empathize with others.

BEFORE READING

Talk to the readers about what makes them happy and any physical changes they notice in their bodies when they feel happy.

Discuss: Name something that makes you happy. How does your body feel when you are happy?

AFTER READING

Talk to the readers about changes that take place in the brain when they feel happy.

Discuss: What happens in your brain when you feel happy? What is one way you can help yourself feel happier?

SEL GOAL

Children may struggle with processing their emotions, and they may lack accessible tools to help them do so. Explain to children that changes take place in their brains when they feel strong emotions. These changes can affect how their bodies feel. Taking certain actions can trigger changes in the brain that make them feel good.

TABLE OF CONTENTS

CHAPTER 1
Feeling Good 4

CHAPTER 2
A Happy Brain 8

CHAPTER 3
Staying Happy and Calm 18

GOALS AND TOOLS
Grow with Goals 22
Try This! 22
Glossary 23
To Learn More 23
Index 24

FEELING GOOD

What makes you feel happy? Maybe you feel happy when you hear your favorite song or spend time with a good friend. For some, going for a bike ride makes them feel good.

Happiness is an **emotion**. You feel happy when you do things that bring you joy. When you feel happy, you might smile or laugh.

Feeling happy can give your body more **energy**. You might even jump for joy! Other times, you might feel relaxed and calm.

CHAPTER 2

A HAPPY BRAIN

When you are happy, changes take place in your brain. Your brain is like a control center. It controls how you think and act in response to what happens around you. When you do something that makes you happy, like hug someone, your brain makes oxytocin.

Oxytocin is a **neurotransmitter**. Your hypothalamus makes this chemical. Oxytocin can make you feel calm. It may make you less **stressed**. It also helps us build relationships. How? It helps us trust and **empathize**.

hypothalamus

midbrain

pituitary gland

How does it work in your brain?

1. Oxytocin is created in the hypothalamus.

2. It travels to the pituitary gland.

3. The pituitary gland releases the chemical. It leaves your brain and enters your blood.

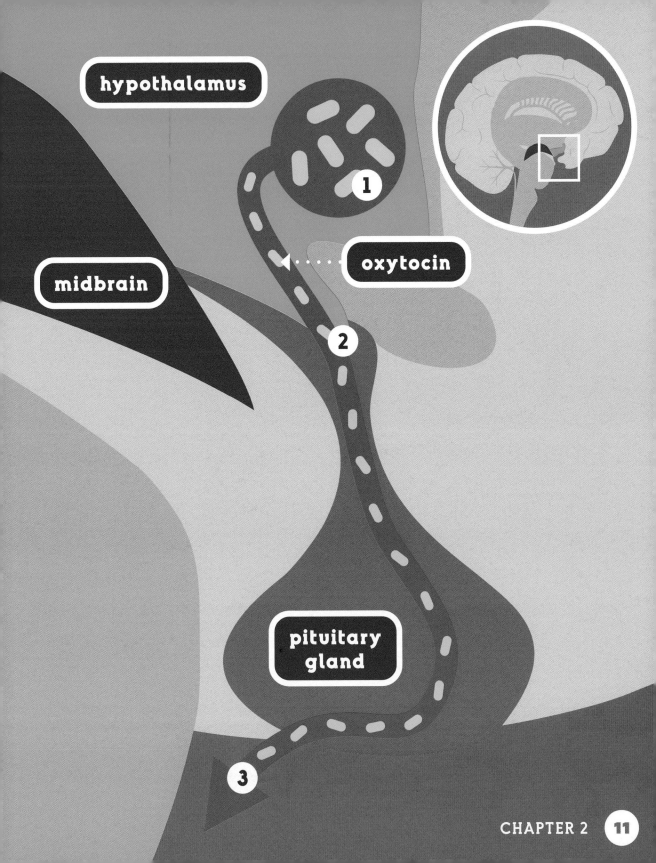

When you do something that makes you feel **rewarded**, like learning to play a new song, your brain makes dopamine. This chemical is made in the midbrain.

Dopamine travels through the rest of your brain. It makes you feel excited and happy. It can also help you focus and stay **motivated**.

PRACTICE HAPPINESS

When you practice something, you get better at it. Your brain works the same way. When you do things that make you happy over and over, your brain gets better at making happy chemicals.

When you do things like exercise, dance, laugh, or listen to music you like, your brain makes **endorphins**. These come from your hypothalamus and pituitary gland. They connect to **receptors** in your brain. This makes you feel pleasure. It also helps you feel less pain and stress.

GET MOVING

Studies show that people who exercise are happier. How? Moving creates more chemical reactions in the brain. Even a short walk can help keep you happy.

Serotonin is another neurotransmitter. Your brain and body make serotonin. The right amount can boost your mood. It also helps you sleep well.

HAPPY AND HEALTHY

Some neurotransmitters make you feel good right away. Others work more slowly. Over time, happiness can help keep your body healthy. Your heart beats more regularly. You sleep better. Happiness can even boost your **immune system!**

STAYING HAPPY AND CALM

No one is happy all the time. Things will happen that make you sad, scared, or angry. You can do things like exercise or spend time with friends to help your brain send happy messages.

Feeling happy takes practice. Try slowing down. Pay close attention. What do you see, hear, and smell around you? This is one way to practice **mindfulness**.

You can also focus on what you are **thankful** for. Thinking about what is good in your life can help you feel happy.

When you're happy, it helps those around you feel the same. Laugh with a friend or smile at your neighbor. These are great ways to share happiness.

JUST SMILE

Scientists study what happens when you smile. Even if you don't feel happy, the act of smiling can cause changes in your brain to make you feel happy.

GOALS AND TOOLS

GROW WITH GOALS

Understanding changes that take place in your brain can help you take charge of your emotions and help you feel good.

Goal: Make a list of activities that help you feel happy. Next time you're feeling down, choose an activity from the list and do it!

Goal: Develop happiness habits. Pick something you can do every day that helps you feel happy. Write it down so you don't forget.

Goal: Spread happiness. Ask others what helps them feel happy.

TRY THIS!

Make a happiness journal. Collect pictures and sayings that you like. Write down stories that make you feel good. Include a list of your favorite songs and what you are thankful for. Add to it over time. Look through the journal when you need a boost of happiness.

GLOSSARY

emotion
A feeling, such as happiness, sadness, or anger.

empathize
To understand and be sensitive to the thoughts and feelings of others.

endorphins
Substances created by the brain that reduce pain and cause pleasant feelings.

energy
The ability or strength to do things without getting tired.

immune system
The system that protects your body against disease and infection.

mindfulness
A mentality achieved by focusing on the present moment and calmly recognizing and accepting your feelings, thoughts, and sensations.

motivated
Having a strong desire to do well at something.

neurotransmitter
A body's chemical messenger that sends information from one neuron to another.

receptors
Nerve endings in your body that react to changes and make your body respond in a particular way.

rewarded
Feeling satisfied or encouraged.

stressed
Experiencing mental or emotional strain.

thankful
Showing thanks or gratitude.

TO LEARN MORE

FACT SURFER

Finding more information is as easy as 1, 2, 3.

1. Go to www.factsurfer.com

2. Enter "**yourbrainwhenyou'rehappy**" into the search box.

3. Choose your book to see a list of websites.

INDEX

blood 10

body 7, 16

brain 8, 10, 12, 15, 16, 18, 20

calm 7, 9

dopamine 12

emotion 5

empathize 9

endorphins 15

energy 7

exercise 15, 18

focus 12, 20

hypothalamus 9, 10, 11, 15

laugh 5, 15, 20

midbrain 9, 11, 12

mindfulness 19

neurotransmitter 9, 16

oxytocin 8, 9, 10, 11

pituitary gland 9, 10, 11, 15

practice 12, 19

receptors 15

rewarded 12

serotonin 16

smile 5, 20

trust 9

Blue Owl Books are published by Jump!, 5357 Penn Avenue South, Minneapolis, MN 55419, www.jumplibrary.com

Copyright © 2023 Jump! International copyright reserved in all countries. No part of this book may be reproduced in any form without written permission from the publisher.

Library of Congress Cataloging-in-Publication Data
Names: Colich, Abby, author.
Title: Your brain when you're happy / by Abby Colich.
Description: Minneapolis, MN: Jump!, Inc., [2023]
Series: Brainpower | Includes index.
Audience: Ages 7–10
Identifiers: LCCN 2022021517 (print)
LCCN 2022021518 (ebook)
ISBN 9798885241434 (hardcover)
ISBN 9798885241441 (paperback)
ISBN 9798885241458 (ebook)
Subjects: LCSH: Happiness in children–Juvenile literature. | Happiness–Juvenile literature. | Happiness–Physiological aspects–Juvenile literature. | Brain–Juvenile literature.
Classification: LCC BF723.H37 C65 2023 (print)
LCC BF723.H37 (ebook)
DDC 152.4/2–dc23/eng/20220608
LC record available at https://lccn.loc.gov/2022021517
LC ebook record available at https://lccn.loc.gov/2022021518

Editor: Eliza Leahy
Designer: Emma Bersie

Photo Credits: Tatyana Vyc/Shutterstock, cover; joephotostudio/Shutterstock, 1; Studio concept/Shutterstock, 3; Monkey Business Images/Shutterstock, 4; narikan/Shutterstock, 5; Sergey Novikov/Shutterstock, 6–7; Dragon Images/Shutterstock, 8; Ranta Images/Shutterstock, 9; Prostock-Studio/iStock, 12–13; AzmanL/iStock, 14–15; Africa Studio/Shutterstock, 16–17; annebaek/iStock, 18; Marcus Lindstrom/iStock, 19; Brocreative/Shutterstock, 20–21.

Printed in the United States of America at Corporate Graphics in North Mankato, Minnesota.